Butterfly

Patterns for Craftspeople and Artisans

JILLIAN SAWYER

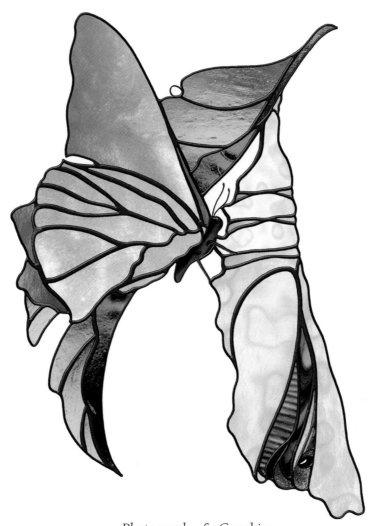

Photography & Graphics
WAYNE McONIE

Published by
GLASS BOOKS PTY LTD

Printed in Western Australia

Dedicated to the beauty of life and my Mum.

STUFF YOU NEED TO KNOW

These butterflies are not biologically accurate, in that nature's markings are nigh on impossible to reproduce in glass without using hundreds of pieces.

Also, the butterflies have not been posed with their food plants; instead I have chosen to place them with plants that will impact with their colour and form.

As usual, use your glass like an artist's palette. I choose glass which has interesting colour variations and even imperfections, as you can use these faults with great impact. Utilize colour, streaks, grain and flow to best effect.

WIREWORK has sometimes been placed for design enhancement and often used as extra support in a piece that would otherwise be weak in that area. IT IS VERY IMPORTANT that all wires are soldered into seams where they touch, overlap or even wrap around or under!

FOR EASE OF CONSTRUCTION A SIZE OF 300 to 600mm (12 to 24 inches) is recommended.

As with *Frog Song* I have taken the liberty of placing smaller butterflies throughout.

National Library of Australia Cataloguing-in-Publication entry

Sawyer, Jillian.
Butterfly.

ISBN 0 9581988 0 2.

1. Glass craft - Patterns. 2. Glass painting and staining - Patterns. 3. Decoration and ornament - Animal forms.
4. Decoration and ornament - Plant forms. 5. Butterflies in art. I. McOnie, Wayne. II. Title.

748.5

Published by Glass Books Pty Ltd
PO Box 891 Subiaco Western Australia 6904
info@glassbooks.com.au
www.glassbooks.com.au

November 2003
Reprinted April 2005

FOREWORD

A furry brown caterpillar crawling over my hands, or curling up in a ball to play dead if I poked it, then slowly uncurling and undulating away when it felt safe. Trying to catch butterflies without a net, this was relatively easy with the bigger, slower ones. Never did catch a little skipper though, even after patiently following them all over the back lawn, too fast for me!

Who didn't play with caterpillars or chase butterflies when they were a child?

The common butterflies that visited my childhood were yellows, whites, black and whites, browns and oranges and, of course, the little skippers and blues. I don't remember that we ever had names for them, they were just beautiful butterflies.

We also kept silkworms as kids; they spent their whole lives in shoe boxes with holes punched in the lids for ventilation. I remember we used to feed them different greens for different coloured silks. My girlfriend and I used to clamber onto her shed's roof and pinch her neighbour's mulberry leaves for pink silk. Of course, we'd have a good feed while we were up there and come down faces, hands, pinnies and clothes stained pink from the yummy mulberries. The worms were regular eating machines and when they spun their cocoons we waited patiently for metamorphosis and the moths to appear.

Metamorphosis – now there's a word! We usually use it to describe the change of a caterpillar to a butterfly, or a tadpole to a frog, but how apt a word to describe our own life changes: The gradual change from baby to adult, the transition of girl to beautiful woman, boy to fine young man and of youth giving way to age. The change of a bud to flower then fruit. The change of form or structure during any natural life. The change of the world around us.

After all, isn't all life about change? Change in appearance, character and circumstances?

The caterpillar just does it in a far quicker and more spectacular way.

The Butterfly.

JILLIAN SAWYER

PO Box 522
Cannington
Western Australia 6107
Email: firebird@iinet.net.au

FOOTNOTE: In these pieces you will notice I have had a love affair with the beautiful iridised glass that is available to us now. It is extremely difficult to photograph and nearly drove Wayne up the wall. He resorted to all sorts of trickery and manipulation!

ULYSSES ON ORCHID

DANAUS ON POPPY

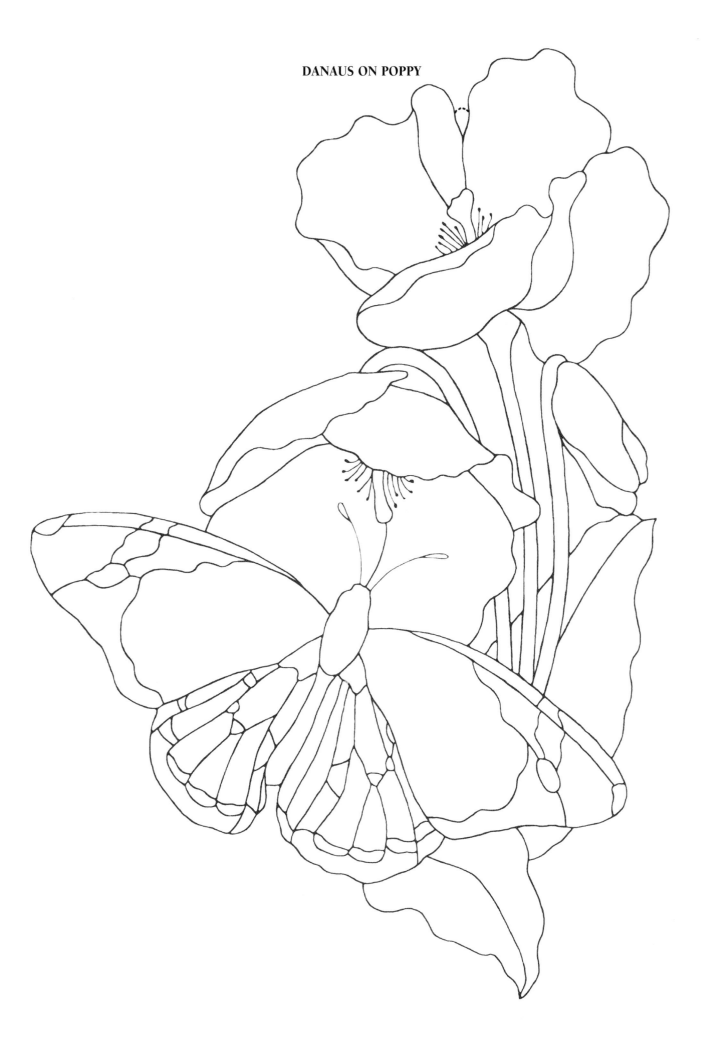

ADMIRAL

GOLD KENYA

FRITILLARY

BUTTERFLY

Beautiful thing on fragile wing
What part do you play in Creation's story?
Oh wondrous sight in beautiful flight
When your wings shine in all their glory
It is then I am sure you were sent to beguile
To entrance and delight and to make us all smile.

8

TOUCHED BY A BUTTERFLY

*She flew in the car window one day, her colours so cheerful
and bright and landed on his shoulder. He said "Wow honey,
take a look at this!" Very gently she stepped onto my finger
from her strong perch and stayed there awhile, until I put her
on the seat beside me.*

*She travelled with us for a half hour or more and I wondered
if she were nearing the end of her life, she was so still.*

*Reaching our destination, she came onto my finger once more
and I gently lowered her to the grass. Joy of joys, she took to
flight, fluttering off on her way, her journey through life
obviously not finished yet.*

*We will forever remember the honour of her company and the
wonder she bought to us that day.*

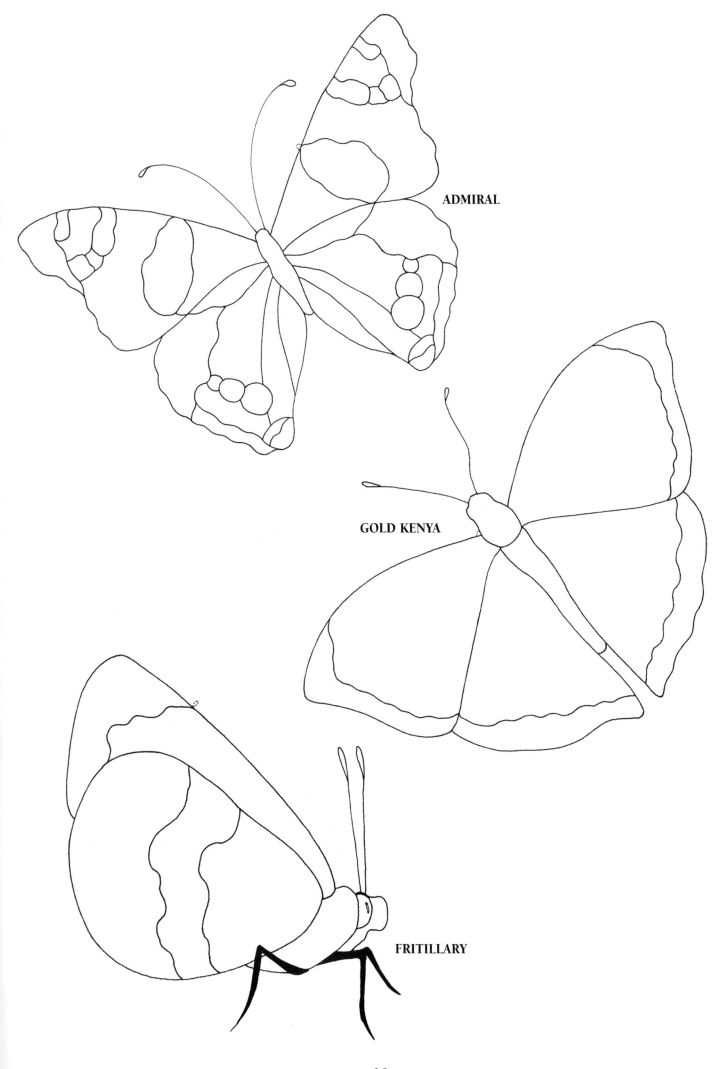

ADMIRAL

GOLD KENYA

FRITILLARY

10

BUTTERFLY LADY

Beautiful Butterfly Lady from the golden age of time
An age of happiness and innocence, when nature flourished sublime
They came to you when you called them, fluttering from afar
Alighting on your forehead, anointing it with nectar
You were blessed with more than their beauty, their gentle touch and their grace
You were blessed for the rest of eternity and it shows in your beautiful face.

ROSE SWALLOWTAIL

Rose Swallowtail on a fuchsia, a sight not too often seen
With your pretty rose coloured markings matching the fuchsia's pink sheen
And the fuchsias dancing below you as if they could take to the wing
To me it's a symphony and harmony, of colours that really do sing.

BUTTERFLY LADY

Antennae: Front – wire curled around to form eye
before becoming antenna. Back – crossing over and
soldered to become hanging loop.
Legs: Cut line into forehead – overlay onto body.
Eyebrows: Cut line through forehead and around
bottom of jewel.
Eyes, nostrils and mouth: Painted.
Necklace antennae: Wire overlay.

ROSE SWALLOWTAIL ON FUCHSIA

Antennae: Attached tinned copper wire.
Proboscis: Thin wire overlay, twisted to shape and attached.
Legs: Bent thicker gauge tinned copper wire overlays.
Stems: Thick copper wire.
Stamen: Tinned copper sheet shapes and solder blobs over and under.

Hanging loop taken into seam.
Top Butterfly
Antennae and legs: Tinned coppersheet cut to shape and attached where overlapping.
Butterfly Trio Forming Flower
Antennae: Tinned copperwire with solder blobs, attached at every overlapping point.

Antennae: Overlaid wire
attached at two points
each on head.

LUNA MOTH

MOTHER OF PEARL MOTH

MOON MOTHS

21

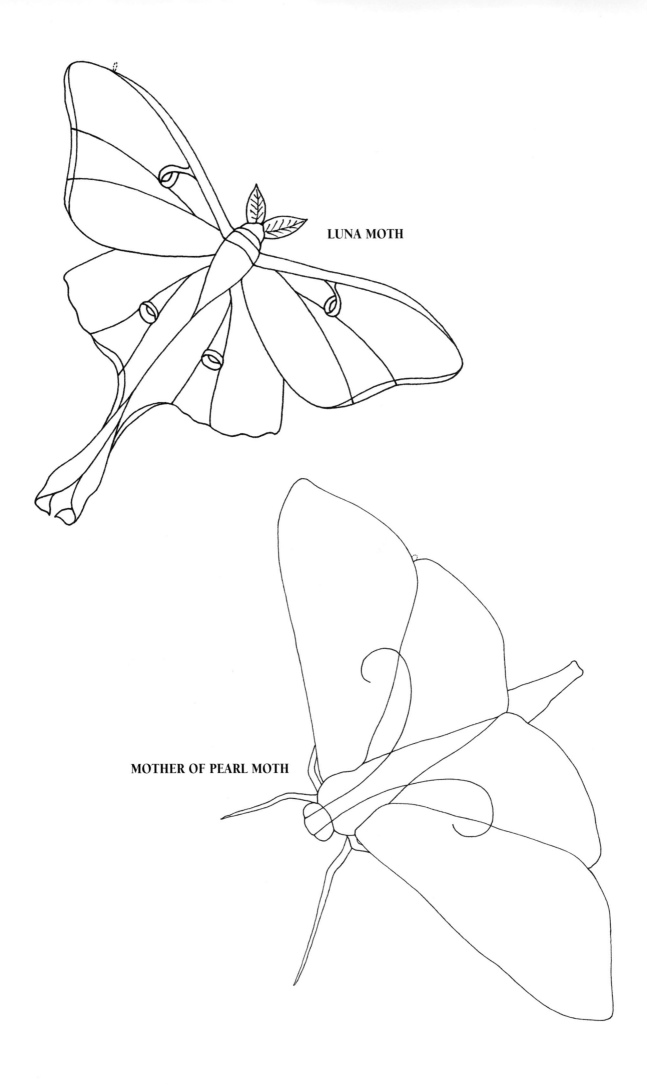

LUNA MOTH

MOTHER OF PEARL MOTH

RAJAH BROOKE'S BIRDWING ON ORCHID

COMMON BIRDWING ON CORDYLINE

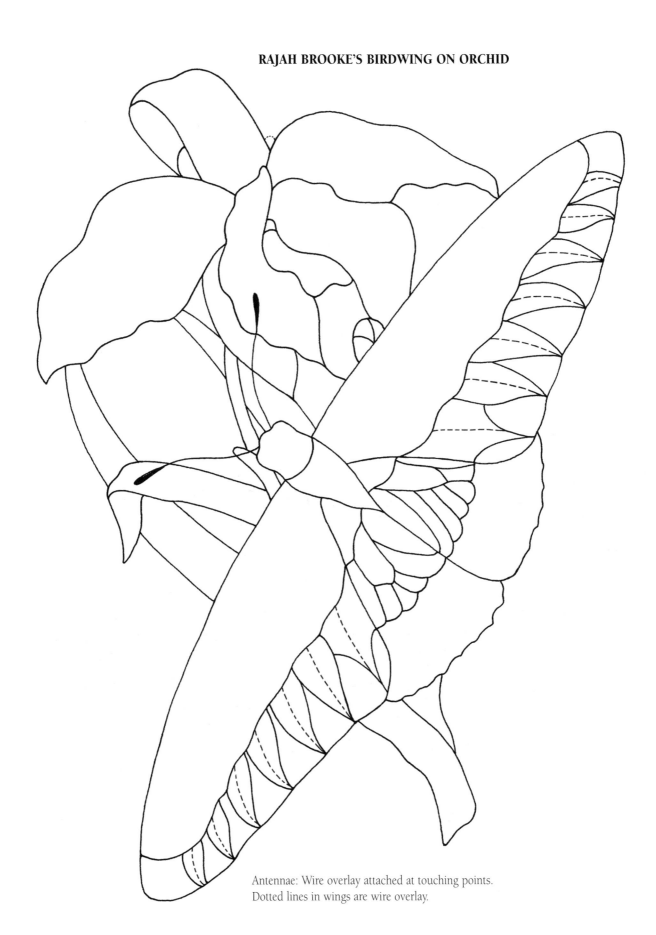

Antennae: Wire overlay attached at touching points.
Dotted lines in wings are wire overlay.

Antennae: Wire overlay attached at touching points.

THE BUTTERFLY BALL
All dressed up and wings aquiver
Excitement builds and hearts aflutter
Anticipation in our eyes does glitter
What do you think is our feelings source?
We're off to the Butterfly Ball, of course!

THE MASK
Well, now here we be and so, you can see,
I've chosen to masquerade.
Incognito this way, I'll be bright and gay
And maybe my match will be made.

ALICE

Antennae: Attached at
head and taken into seam.
Eyelash: Attached wire at
appropriate position.
Earring: Butterfly's
antennae are overlaid
copperwire.

JANINE

Antennae: Cut line to hair and then overlaid.
Nostrils and mouth: Painted.
Eyelashes: Wire overlay.
Eyes: Glass teddy bear eyes.

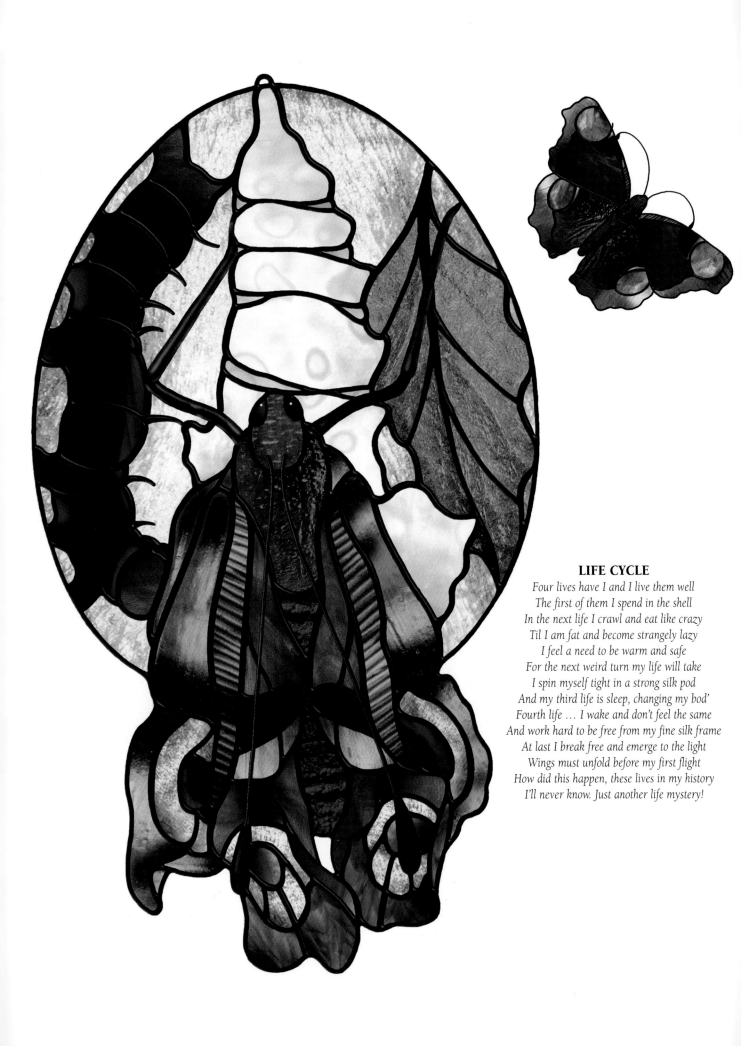

LIFE CYCLE

Four lives have I and I live them well
The first of them I spend in the shell
In the next life I crawl and eat like crazy
Til I am fat and become strangely lazy
I feel a need to be warm and safe
For the next weird turn my life will take
I spin myself tight in a strong silk pod
And my third life is sleep, changing my bod'
Fourth life … I wake and don't feel the same
And work hard to be free from my fine silk frame
At last I break free and emerge to the light
Wings must unfold before my first flight
How did this happen, these lives in my history
I'll never know. Just another life mystery!

SPANISH MOON MOTH

Like a Flamenco dancers' dress swirling bright
Spanish Moonmoth dances at night
Wings fluttering, catch the moon beams
So pretty a sight, such beautiful greens
On you dance, following nights' scent
To mate in soft light, before night is spent.

Hanging loop into seams.
Caterpillar spines: Middle one cut line, others tinned sheet copper overlaid and attached at back segments.
Antennae: Overlaid wire to glass teardrop shapes at end and attached at head and to seams where crossing (stand proud from seams).
Legs: Overlaid thick gauge wire attached at appropriate points.

Antennae: Wire wrapped foiled glass
attached at head and taken into seams.

BUCKEYE

PEACOCK

SCARCE COPPER ON CANTERBURY BELLS

BUCKEYE

PEACOCK

38

SCARCE COPPER ON CANTERBURY BELLS

THE VISITOR

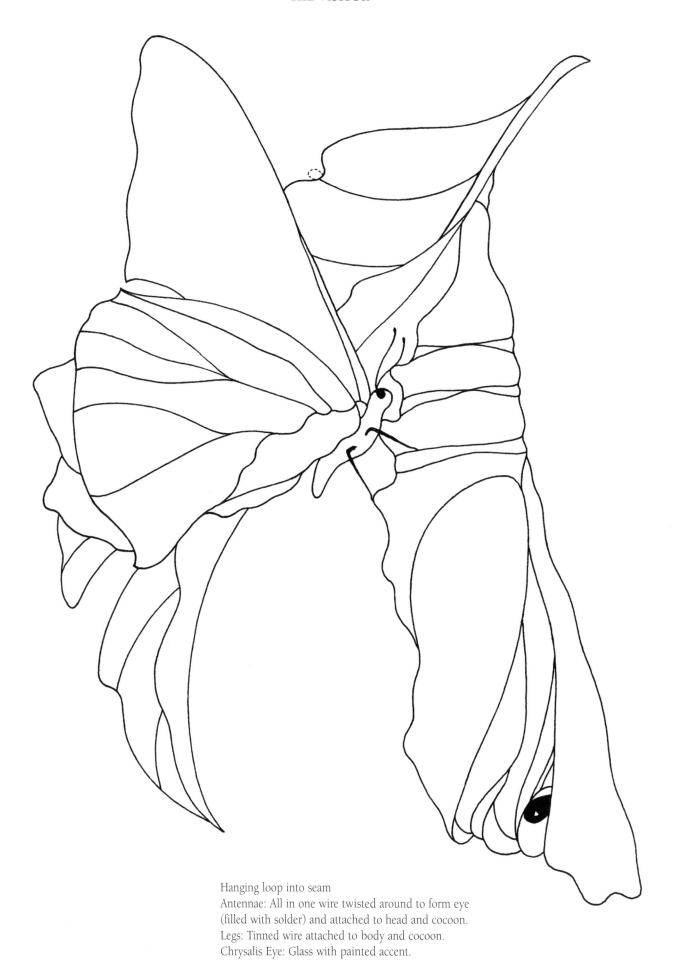

Hanging loop into seam
Antennae: All in one wire twisted around to form eye
(filled with solder) and attached to head and cocoon.
Legs: Tinned wire attached to body and cocoon.
Chrysalis Eye: Glass with painted accent.

Hanging loop: Wire taken into seam and attached at all overlaid points.

Antennae: Cut line and wire overlay onto branches.

Twig next to right antennae: Cut line and wire overlay onto butterfly wing.

Vine (above wing): Wire into seam and then twisted and attached at appropriate points.

Vine (below wing): Wire on edge and then overlaid onto leaves.

Crystal hanging loop: Wire buried in seam on twig then round edge and attached at all points where running under glass.

SWALLOWTAIL DAISY

PURPLE-SHOT COPPER

OAK BLUE

SWALLOWTAIL DAISY

Hanging loop buried in seam, taken along top
of petal, twisted to form loop, continued
along top and buried into opposite seam.
Antennae: Cut line underneath then overlaid
and twisted to form eye (solder filled) and
other antennae.
All legs overlaid.

PURPLE-SHOT COPPER

OAK BLUE

47

BUTTERFLIES IN MY GARDEN

There's a butterfly or two in my garden, sipping the sweet cottage flowers.
White ones on lavender, brown ones on daisies, peacocks on sweet honesty.
Orange spots hover near dear granny bonnets, tucked right away over there
And I'm sure I can see that they all love old fashioned posies
Just a little like old fashioned me.

HIGH PRIESTESS

Because life is precious to her, she waits.
When nature has taken its course, she gathers the
golden butterfly wings and uses their essence to
perform her sacred rite.
She sees the future looming ever closer in the light.
Two paths open before her, one showing death and
destruction, the other beauty and life.
She knows the nature of mankind; she knows the
choices we make.
Now the time is upon us, when the hard choices
must be made. What price the cost of progress at
the expense of beauty and life?
She knows the nature of mankind, so she knows
the path she must take.
She waits.

ORANGE SPOTS ON COLUMBINES

Dotted lines are wire overlay.

HIGH PRIESTESS

Antennae: Overlaid wire.
Butterfly eye: Soldered to head with overlaid coiled wire.
Legs: Overlaid thick gauge wire or tinned copper sheet.
Eyelash: Overlaid wire into seam.
Lip lines: Overlaid wire, except for middle, which is cut line.
Proboscis: Wire buried into seam and coiled and attached over forehead.

FLITTERBUGS
More jewel-like critters!
They love to flitter
All round your windows each day
So make their wings shimmer
If you like, make them glimmer
In fact, do them all your own way.

FLUTTERBYS

Another fun, stubby squadron
Is fluttering in to greet you
To get rid of your present doldrum
And giving you heaps more to do.

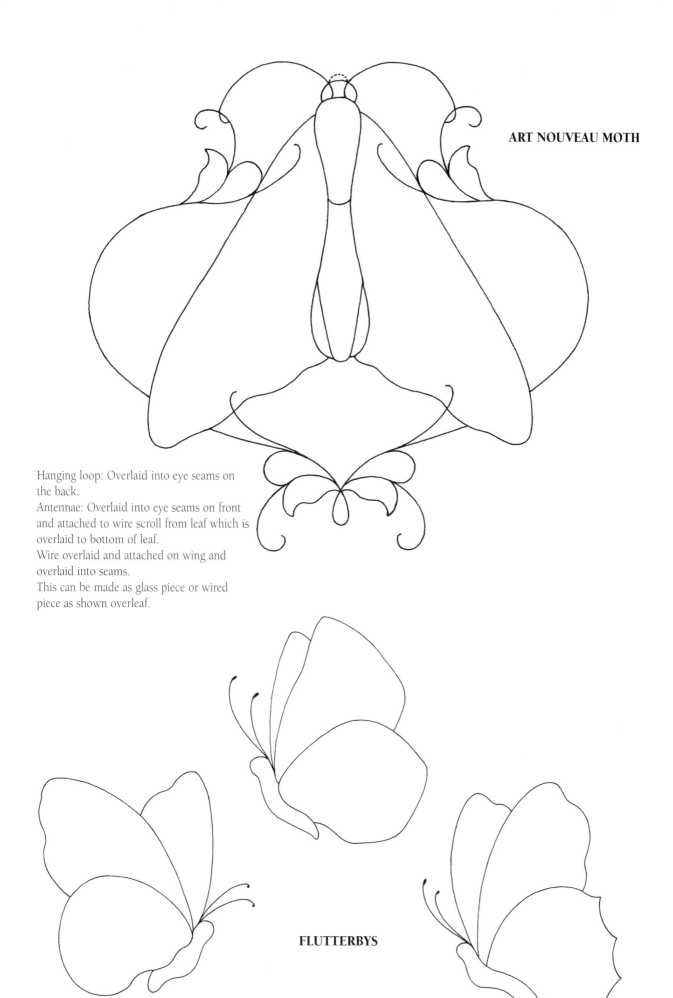

ART NOUVEAU MOTH

Hanging loop: Overlaid into eye seams on
the back.
Antennae: Overlaid into eye seams on front
and attached to wire scroll from leaf which is
overlaid to bottom of leaf.
Wire overlaid and attached on wing and
overlaid into seams.
This can be made as glass piece or wired
piece as shown overleaf.

FLUTTERBYS

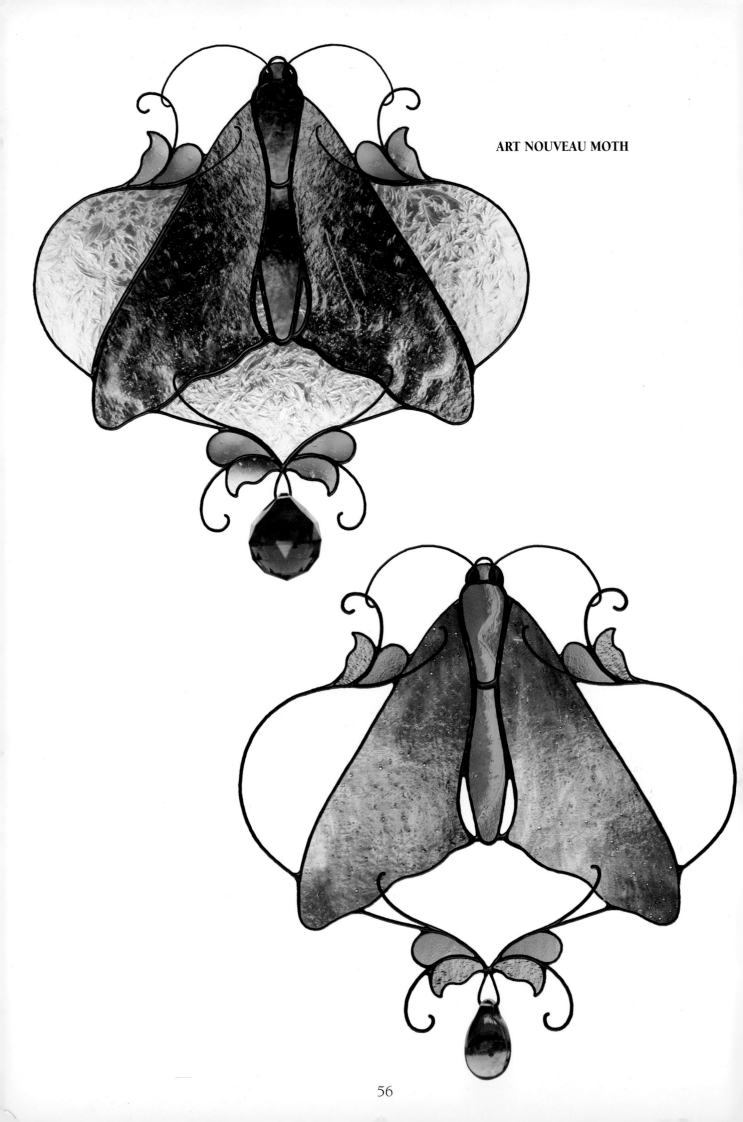

ART NOUVEAU MOTH

56